ONLY PASSING THROUGH

The Story of Sojourner Truth

CHILDREN WHO MADE IT NOT GOD? WHO MADE THE SAME GOD? AM BECAUSE MY SKIN IS BLA REPROACH ON OUR MAKER CHILDREN BECAUSE HE THEM A BLACK SKIN? INDE YOUR TEACHERS OUGHT UP IF POSSIBLE THE GREA COLOR FROM YOUR MIND WHAT SOSOURNER TRUTH

OUR SKIN WHITE? WAS
MINE BLACK? WAS IT NOT
TO BLAME THEREFORE
? DOES IT NOT CAST A
O DESPISE A PART OF HIS
BEEN PLEASED TO GIVE
CHILDREN IT DOES. AND
TELL YOU SO AND ROOT
IN OF PRESUDICE AGAINST
NOW CHILDREN REMEMBER
AS TOLD YOU.

ONLY PASSING THROUGH

The Story of Sojourner Truth

by Anne Rockwell   illustrated by R. Gregory Christie

Dragonfly Books —⚬— New York

Strangers stared while the auctioneer poked and pointed at the girl with his stick—showing how tall and strong she was. He promised that since she was only about nine years old and already so tall, she'd soon be able to do the work of any man.

The girl's owner had died, and his property, which included a few slaves, was being auctioned off to pay his debts. Her mother and father weren't being sold, for they were old and sick. No one would want them. They'd been set free to look after themselves. Her father, who'd been as tall and strong as a tree, was bent and lame with arthritis. He could hardly walk, let alone work for a living.

Young, tall, and strong as she was, no one bid for the slave girl called Isabella at that auction in Kingston, New York, in 1806. The sun settled low in the sky and still she wasn't sold. Finally the auctioneer offered to throw in a flock of sheep if someone would just buy the girl so he could call it a day and go home for supper.

Then a farmer did.

She didn't understand a word her new owner said. He spoke English and she spoke Dutch, as nearly everyone living along the Hudson River did in those days. He whipped her when she didn't understand what she'd been ordered to do. He whipped her so hard that blood flowed down her back. Isabella earned her first words of English with scars that remained all her life.

After two years, she was sold to a Dutch-speaking man who owned a tavern down by the river. She eavesdropped on the rough boatmen and sleigh drivers who came there to eat and drink. Many spoke English. She paid careful attention to their words, memorizing new ones every day.

When she turned thirteen, a neighboring farmer offered the tavern keeper a good price for her.

Isabella's new owner was English-speaking, but by now she spoke and understood his language. She liked John Dumont more than her other masters. She was sure he liked her, too, for he often told her she was the best bargain he'd ever made.

By the time she was sixteen, Isabella was six feet tall and could do the work of any man, just as the auctioneer had promised. She was also old enough to have children, who'd be slaves for Dumont. So her master gave her to one of his other slaves, an older man named Thomas, to be his wife.

Isabella wouldn't have chosen Thomas for a husband, had she been given a choice. But slaves didn't have a choice in such matters.

She and Thomas had four daughters and a son. Every night, Isabella prayed Dumont wouldn't sell them to an owner who lived far away, as had happened to her brother and sister.

Isabella's mother had often told the story of the morning when her little boy and girl had raced from the dark cellar where they and the other slaves lived. They'd heard the jingling of sleigh bells and were eager to investigate. The stranger driving the sleigh had grabbed the children, shoved them into a box, locked it, then driven off. But he couldn't shut the box tight enough to keep their terrified screams from drowning out the bells as the sleigh raced over bright, new-fallen snow.

Her mother never told the story without breaking down in sobs. Her parents never stopped grieving for their lost children. And their pain became Isabella's own. It was something they passed on to her just as surely as her father passed on his great height and strength.

Sometimes she wondered what it would be like not to have to dread such things. When Isabella was alone, she looked to the stars, for that was where her mother had told her God lived—God, who looked out for the long-lost children, wherever they were, and Isabella, too. She often talked to God and believed she heard Him answer. Sometimes she'd ask if a day would ever come when she would be free.

One day, an answer came—not from God but from John Dumont. In 1825, when Isabella was twenty-eight years old, Dumont told her that he'd decided to reward her for her hard work by freeing her in a year.

She didn't know his offer wasn't as generous as it sounded. In fact, he was required to set her free in two years. Slavery was gradually ending in New York. A state law had been passed in 1817 decreeing that most adult slaves were to be set free on the Fourth of July, 1827. Dumont knew that—but Isabella didn't.

From the day he made his promise, Isabella thought of nothing but her coming freedom day. She had a beautiful singing voice and sang out with joy every morning, for each day that passed brought the great one nearer.

But then Isabella cut her right hand on a scythe and couldn't work in the fields. When her dreamed-of freedom day finally came, Dumont said that since she hadn't done enough work for him in the past year, he figured she owed him another year's worth of work.

Isabella was devastated that the master she'd trusted would betray her. She couldn't allow him to do this.

She spent the next few days spinning every last bit of wool that had been sheared from Dumont's sheep. She planned to leave no work undone. She'd leave no reason her children could be punished in her place.

Isabella didn't sleep at all the night she finished spinning. Before the sun rose, she walked away from the farm, taking for herself the freedom Dumont had promised her.

A few miles away lived a couple named Isaac and Maria Van Wagener. Isabella had heard that they believed it was immoral to own slaves. She asked if she could board with them and work for wages wherever she could. The Van Wageners said yes.

Dumont came looking for her. He didn't have to look far. He'd already guessed where he'd find her. When he demanded that Isabella come back to the farm with him, Isaac Van Wagener knew the law was on Dumont's side. He acted quickly, offering to buy her for twenty dollars.

Dumont pocketed the money and left.

As soon as he was gone, Isaac told Isabella he'd bought her only so Dumont couldn't take her back. He knew that Isabella would have been cruelly punished for running away, made an example to other slaves. So he'd bought her, even though he knew no human being had the right to own another. Now he was setting her free.

Isabella wept with joy. Her dreamed-of freedom day had come! It was a few days late, but it had come.

It may have been from Isaac or Maria that Isabella first heard Bible stories. She was deeply moved by them, especially the one about Moses leading his people out of bondage in Egypt. He had succeeded; he had set those slaves free! Isabella saw how tragic things that had happened to people could be turned into stories that gave strength and inspiration to others. She began to believe that strong words such as those in the Bible had a power as great as any master's whip.

The Van Wagener farm wasn't far from Dumont's, so Isabella was able to visit her children. One day, she discovered that her five-year-old son, Peter, was gone.

What she'd long dreaded had happened. Dumont had sold Peter. The man who bought him then sold the child to a plantation owner in Alabama. It was against the law in New York to sell a slave out of state. The man who had sold the little boy knew that but figured he could get away with it. After all, who was going to stop him?

But he didn't know that the Van Wageners had been telling Isabella about many laws of the state and country in which she'd been born. She knew that what Peter's new master had done was illegal. She made up her mind to go to court and have her child brought back to New York, where he belonged. She found a lawyer who agreed to help her.

As she stepped into the courtroom to plead her cause, Isabella felt a strange new sensation. Later she told people that she felt "the power of a nation" swelling within her that day in the courthouse.

She won. People for miles around spoke of little else but how a former slave had taken a white man to court, and won. No one had ever heard of such a thing. Slaves didn't do such things. Women didn't do such things. But Isabella did.

Peter was ordered brought back from Alabama and placed in his mother's care. Isabella found his back covered with bloody wounds from a whip—wounds too much like her own.

In 1829, she went to New York City, where she hoped to make enough money to send Peter to school. She'd heard of a school there that black children could attend. She'd seen what words written down in books could do. Words in law books had set her and Peter free. Words in the Bible had touched the deepest places in her soul. Even though she couldn't read and write herself, she wanted to be sure Peter learned how.

Peter went to school, but in 1841, when he was about eighteen, he took a job as a sailor on a whaling ship. He expected to be gone about three years. He wrote Isabella a few letters from faraway places; then she heard nothing more. She waited, but no letters came. Finally she believed Peter must be dead.

In 1843, Isabella woke from a vivid dream. A voice had told her she must leave New York. It said she was meant to travel around the country telling of her time in bondage—telling people what it meant to be a slave. She had to be a voice for all the silent slaves still in bondage.

It was a powerful call. Isabella was sure it was God telling her to do this.

She had only twenty-five cents, which she put in her apron pocket. She tied her few possessions together into a pillowcase, closed the door behind her, and began walking toward the rising sun.

She crossed from Manhattan to Brooklyn on the ferry, then walked into the green countryside of Long Island. As she walked, memories of her life found words, and many were those she'd first heard in the Bible.

One was "sojourner." Isabella knew it meant someone who was only passing through—staying awhile, then moving on to another place. She now believed that she was meant to be a sojourner, always moving on to spread her message. And she knew she'd never serve any master but the truth.

Isabella became a new woman that day. It was as though the life she'd known up till then belonged to someone else. A new one was beginning. The old life had become a tale to tell, a story to bring freedom to others. Her old name belonged to her old life. From that day on, she was never called Isabella again. Her name was Sojourner Truth.

She crossed Long Island Sound by ferry to Connecticut. Wherever she went, she worked in fields, cleaned houses, did laundry, and told her story to whoever would listen. On her travels, she'd usually find someone willing to read the Bible aloud to her, or write a letter to her children, telling them where she was. She preferred it when children read the Bible to her, for they didn't try to interpret the stories, as adults did. They just let her listen to the words, so that she could decide for herself what meaning they had.

She made her way to Northampton, Massachusetts. There she found a community of abolitionists—people who wanted slavery to be made illegal everywhere in the United States. They invited Sojourner to stay and work with them. They noticed how vivid and powerful her images were, how passionate her convictions were. Her great height and plain, old-fashioned clothes made for a striking and dramatic presence. Her new friends thought many more people should hear her message.

They printed posters advertising a free lecture—a firsthand account of what life as a slave was like. They nailed them to trees and fences, then pitched a huge tent at the base of a hill. They hoped people would come from all around to hear Sojourner Truth speak. And they hoped that at least a few people would leave knowing that slavery was wrong.

On the evening of the gathering, many people did come—too many. Among the mostly curious or compassionate crowd was a gang of young men who'd been drinking whiskey. They carried sticks and shouted that black people were inferior to whites, that no slaves should be free. They'd obviously come looking for a fight and soon threatened to burn down the tent full of people.

It was dangerous for Sojourner to be seen, let alone heard, as long as those men were there. She was the very target the drunken bullies were looking for. She hid behind the tent, and her friends told her to stay there until the constable came to arrest the men.

Sojourner sat huddled in darkness waiting for the shouting and fighting to stop. As she sat shaking with terror, she felt ashamed as well. She wasn't being true to her calling. She couldn't stay hidden like that. She had to find the courage to say what needed to be said.

No one noticed her walking up the hill. As soon as she reached the top, Sojourner began to sing. A big white ball of a moon shone behind her, silhouetting her tall, straight figure. Her voice carried down to where people swarmed, still fighting.

The gang of men ran up the hill, but she went on singing. When they came close to her, swinging their sticks, she paused in her song, gazed steadily at them, then asked why they wanted to hurt her, for she had never hurt them.

To her amazement, they threw down their sticks and promised not to hurt her if she'd only sing some more.

So she sang. Finally she paused and spoke patiently but firmly, as she would to small children. She said she'd sing one more song. But then they must pay attention to what she'd come to tell them. And when she was done speaking, they must go home without any more fighting or arguing.

The tough men who'd come to pick a fight that night promised to do what she asked.

Sojourner Truth found strong words for the message she had to deliver. She stood tall and dignified as a queen while she told many terrible truths about being a slave—of children stolen from their parents, of slaves crowded together in damp and filthy cellars, of masters who died leaving their slaves to the whims of others. She told about her father—a lame old man who froze to death alone in a shack in the woods. She told of beatings whose scars never healed.

But Sojourner also told of the triumphs of taking freedom for herself, of using the law to bring her son back. As she spoke, she felt the power her words had and knew she'd never be afraid to speak before a crowd again.

She made people listen. She made people understand. So when Sojourner Truth finally asked, "Is this any way to treat a human being?" people knew the answer was no.

She wandered for many years, a tall, dark figure in plain gray clothes, wearing a white cap on her head. She'd stop for a while, say what needed saying, then move on. She was a sojourner, only passing through. When people threatened to burn down the place where she planned to speak, she vowed angrily that she'd still be heard, speaking from the ashes. Wherever she went, she carried a white silk banner with the words "Proclaim Liberty" embroidered on it.

People listened and thought about what they had heard.

They told others what Sojourner Truth had said.

And her message spread throughout the land.

AUTHOR'S NOTE

When evil rules a time and place, certain good people are called upon to tell the truth to those who don't want to hear it.

I've always loved stories of people who understood in one miraculous moment exactly what they had to do to confront the evil around them—Moses, Saint Paul, Joan of Arc, Saint Francis of Assisi, Sojourner Truth. Such stories fill me and many others with wonder. They live on and spark our imaginations, as they should.

Sojourner Truth called herself "a self-made woman," but she didn't mean it in any materialistic way. She meant it quite literally—that she had created the free and powerful messenger named Sojourner Truth out of the slave woman Isabella, a person born with no status and no dignity.

Although I used many sources for this book, Sojourner Truth's own autobiography was what I found most helpful. It is there that she told the events of her early life that inspired the story I've told.

I've told her story only up to when her transformation took place, for that part of the story moves me most. But there is more to tell of Sojourner Truth's life. On her long journey, she crossed paths with many of the great people of her time—Abraham Lincoln, Frederick Douglass, Lucretia Mott. I hope readers will go on to find out more about her and the times she lived in.

After the Civil War ended, she still spoke out for the many slaves who'd been set free into a world that wasn't prepared for them. She also spoke out for women, who were denied the rights men had. For she saw that even decent men who knew that slavery was evil weren't troubled that all women—including their wives, mothers, sisters, and daughters—were denied the rights they took for granted.

She was a guide for her time and ours. When her old legs were tired from wandering, she insisted upon riding one of the streetcars of Washington, D.C., that only white people rode. I believe she was the first African American to demand, and win, the right to board public transportation along with white people, but she certainly wasn't the last.

In 1883, when she was dying, Sojourner told friends and family who had come to say good-bye not to cry. She told them she was going home, "like a shooting star." She'd always looked to the night sky, finding comfort and guidance there, as her mother had taught her. Her time on earth had been long. Now it was time to stop wandering. It was time to go home.

More than a hundred years after her death, the United States launched a small vehicle to explore the surface of Mars. A competition was held among schoolchildren to give the Mars rover a name. A girl from Bridgeport, Connecticut, won the competition, and the name she chose was perfect.

The rover is named after another American wanderer—one who always looked to the stars. It is called "Sojourner."

The nineteenth century was a time of tragic conflict for the United States. Although the young nation had been founded on the ideals of freedom and equality, the fact that many of its people were slaves contradicted these ideals. No women had rights equal to men's. Change was in the air and had to come.

Sojourner Truth, Frederick Douglass, and Harriet Tubman were three former slaves who said and did much to bring about the end of slavery. Lucretia Mott, Susan B. Anthony, and Elizabeth Cady Stanton worked to change the plight of women. Sojourner Truth saw the justice of their cause and added her voice to theirs. Here are some of the events that took place during Sojourner Truth's long life:

797? Bett and Baumfree, slaves of a man named Charles Ardinburgh in Ulster County, New York, have a daughter named Isabella.

826   Isabella is freed.

828   Isabella successfully sues a white man for illegally selling her son Peter out of state.

843   Isabella leaves New York City and becomes Sojourner Truth. She begins to roam New England, telling of her life as a slave.

845   Frederick Douglass, an escaped slave, writes his autobiography.

848   Lucretia Mott and Elizabeth Cady Stanton organize the first Women's Rights Convention, in Seneca Falls, New York.

849   Harriet Tubman escapes from slavery and leads many other slaves to freedom via the Underground Railroad.

850   Sojourner Truth dictates her autobiography. She speaks at the first national Women's Rights Convention, in Worcester, Massachusetts. She is the only black person present.

1860 Abraham Lincoln is elected the sixteenth president of the United States. South Carolina secedes from the Union.

1861 Seven more Southern states secede. The Civil War begins.

1863 Lincoln issues the Emancipation Proclamation, freeing all slaves in the rebel states. On the battlefield at Gettysburg, Pennsylvania, Lincoln delivers the Gettysburg Address, stating, "Four score and seven years ago our fathers brought forth on this continent a new nation, conceived in liberty and dedicated to the proposition that all men are created equal."

1864 Sojourner Truth begins to work with the National Freedman's Relief Association in Washington, D.C., set up to help newly freed slaves from the South find shelter and work.

1865 The Civil War ends with victory for the Union. President Lincoln is assassinated. Andrew Johnson becomes president. The Thirteenth Amendment to the Constitution abolishes slavery throughout the United States.

1869 Elizabeth Cady Stanton and Susan B. Anthony found the National Woman Suffrage Association, hoping to win women's rights through an amendment to the Constitution.

1870 The Fifteenth Amendment proclaims that the right of citizens to vote shall not be denied on the basis of race, but the right of women to vote is not included in the amendment.

1878 Eighty-one-year-old Sojourner Truth is a delegate to the Women's Rights Convention in Rochester, New York.

1883 Sojourner Truth dies in Battle Creek, Michigan.

1919 The Nineteenth Amendment gives women the right to vote. None of the women who started the women's rights movement are alive to see this happen.

For Nicholas, Julianna, Nigel, and Christian —A.R.

To Jacquline and Tanja.
Thank you both for your kindness
and friendship in Berlin —R.G.C.

All rights reserved. Published in the United States by Dragonfly Books,
an imprint of Random House Children's Books, a division of Random House, Inc., New York.
Originally published in hardcover in the United States by Alfred A. Knopf,
an imprint of Random House Children's Books, a division of Random House, Inc., New York, in 2000.

Dragonfly Books with the colophon is a registered trademark of Random House, Inc.

Visit us on the Web! www.randomhouse.com/kids

Educators and librarians, for a variety of teaching tools, visit us at
www.randomhouse.com/teachers

Library of Congress Cataloging-in-Publication Data
Rockwell, Anne F.
Only passing through : the story of Sojourner Truth / by Anne Rockwell ; illustrated by R. Gregory Christie.
p.   cm.
ISBN 978-0-679-89186-4 (trade) — ISBN 978-0-679-99186-1 (lib. bdg.) —
ISBN 978-0-440-41766-8 (pbk.)
1. Truth, Sojourner, d. 1883—Juvenile literature. 2. Afro-American abolitionists—Biography—Juvenile literature.
3. Afro-American women—Biography—Juvenile literature. 4. Abolitionists—United States—Biography—Juvenile literature.
5. Social reformers—United States—Biography—Juvenile literature. [1. Truth, Sojourner, d. 1883.
2. Abolitionists. 3. Reformers. 4. Afro-Americans—Biography. 5. Women—Biography.]
I. Christie, R. Gregory, ill. II. Title.
E185.97.T8 R63 2000
305.5'67'092—dc21   [B]
00035736

MANUFACTURED IN CHINA

22

OUR SKIN WHITE? WAS MINE BLACK? WAS IT NOT TO BLAME THEREFORE? DOES IT NOT CAST... TO DESPISE A PART OF HIS... BEEN PLEASED TO GIVE CHILDREN IT DOES. AND... TELL YOU SO AND ROOT... IN OF PREJUDICE AGAINST... NOW CHILDREN. REMEMBER... AS TOLD YOU.